INTRODUCTION:

THIS BOOK IS FOR THE PEOPLE THAT HAVE NEVER TOUCHED A WRENCH AND WANT TO LEARN THE VERY BASICS TO START SAVING MONEY AND GETTING YOUR HANDS DIRTY! (NO PUN INTENDED). I WILL BE GOING THROUGH A FEW TIPS TO KNOW FOR EITHER WORKING ON YOUR CAR OR EVEN JUST MAINTAINING EVEN IF YOU ARENT DOING THE WORK YOURSELF. STAYING INFORMED AND EDUCATED IS BETTER THAN NOTHING!

CONTENTS

-- -- -- -- -- -- -- -- -- -- -- -- -- -- -- --

CHAPTER 1: PREVENTATIVE MAINTENANCE

FIRST THINGS FIRST IS STARTING WITH A GOOD BASE TO KNOW WHAT EVERYTHING IS AND WHY IT IS IMPORTANT TO KEEP THESE THINGS MAINTAINED AND WORKING PROPERLY.

ITEM #1:

ENGINE AIR FILTER:

A COMPONENT PART OF YOUR CARS INTAKE SYSTEM. IT FILTERS COMTAMINANTS FROM OUTSIDE THAT MANY GET INTO YOUR AIRBOX TO PREVENT DAMAGE TO YOUR ENGINE.

ENGINE AIR FILTER ——————————

YOU MAY BE WONDERING WHY CAR DEALERSHIPS WILL ASK YOU TO REPLACE YOUR VEHICLES ENGINE AIR FILTER? IT IS A FAIRLY CHEAP AND INEXPENSIVE MAINTENANCE ITEM, BUT IT CAN BE EASILY MISSED WHICH CAN FOR THE MOST PART AFFECT FUEL ECONOMY (LESS ZOOM ZOOM).

ENGINE AIR FILTER ————————

IF THE FILTER IS DIRTY BUT IT COULD BE CLEANED ENOUGH WITH AIR, THAT WOULD BE RECOMMENDED TO SAVE ANY MONEY. THE FILTER IS JUST A STRUCTURED PIECE OF MATERIAL THAT FILTERS SMALL PARTICLES ENOUGH TO PROTECT THE ENGINE AND ALLOW ONLY FRESH AIR INTO THE ENGINE WITHOUT SACRIFICING TOO MUCH HORSEPOWER.

ENGINE AIR FILTER ⸺

IF YOU FEEL LIKE CHECKING YOUR AIR FILTER, HERE ARE THE STEPS TO DO IT:

FIRST OF ALL, OPEN YOUR HOOD AND LOOK TO WHERE THE INTAKE SIDE OF THE ENGINE WHICH IS TO THE RIGHT ON MOST CARS.

ENGINE AIR FILTER —————

MOST MODERN AIRBOXES ARE HELD ON BY A FEW CLIPS OR LITTLE SCREWS WHICH TAKE LITTLE TO NO EFFORT TO REMOVE. OPEN THE AIRBOX AND REMOVE THE FILTER FROM THE AIRBOX. INSPECT THE FILTER FOR LARGE AMOUNT OF DIRT OR LEAVES. IF THE FILTER WAS BOUGHT WHEN IT WAS WHITE, ANY DISCOLOURATION IS A CLEAR INDICATION TO REPLACE IT.

CHECKING THE BATTERY ——————

THE NEXT ITEM ON THIS LIST IS THE BATTERY. THE BATTERY IS VERY IMPORTANT FOR YOUR CAR TO WORK OR EVEN START, ESPECIALLY WHEN IT STARTS TO GET COLD! *SHIVER*

CHECKING THE BATTERY ———

HOW IS THE BATTERY CONNECTED TO MY CAR? GOOD QUESTION. THE BATTERY IS THE REASON YOUR CAR CAN GET UP AND GOING, LIKE ANYONE AND THEIR DOUBLE DOUBLE FROM TIMS. IT IS CONNECTED FROM TWO TERMINALS, THE RED WIRE WHICH IS KNOWN AS THE POSITIVE SIDE AND THE BLACK WIRE WHICH IS THE NEGATIVE.

CHECKING THE BATTERY

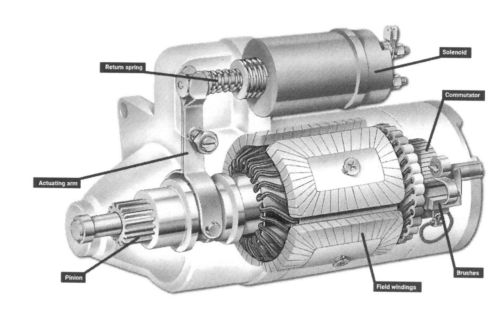

Return spring · Solenoid · Commutator · Actuating arm · Pinion · Field windings · Brushes

THE RED WIRE IS CONNECTED TO THE STARTER (IMAGE ABOVE). THE VOLTAGE COMES FROM THE BATTERY, IN SIMPLE TERMS ACTIVATES THE STARTER MOTOR TO TOUCH GEARS WITH THE FLYWHEEL

CHECKING THE BATTERY ————

THE FLYWHEEL IS A DISC RIVETED WITH GEAR TEETH TO BE DRIVEN BY THE STARTER GEAR WHEN YOU TURN THE KEY. IT TURNS THE ENGINE TO ASSIST IN STARTING ALONG WITH OTHER SYSTEMS WE WILL DISCUSS LATER. ALSO IS USED FOR ENGAGING THE CLUTCH.

CHECKING THE BATTERY ———

NOW THAT YOU UNDERSTAND WHAT A BATTERY DOES, LETS GO TO WHY YOU SHOULD CHECK IT:

YOU SEE THIS CRUSTY SUBSTANCE? THAT IS BATTERY ACID OR SOMETIMES CORROSION. IT HAPPENS WHEN YOUR BATTERY IS DEFECTIVE AND CAN REALLY AFFECT YOUR CAR IN A BAD WAY.

CHECKING THE BATTERY ———

IT CAN EFFECT YOU WHEN YOU NEED YOUR CAR THE MOST, IN THE WINTER! IF YOUR BATTERY CAN'T HOLD CHARGE, YOUR CAR MAY NOT START PROPERLY, OR AT ALL. HERE ARE A FEW WAYS TO PREVENT THIS ------------------

wiki How to Clean Battery Terminals

CHECKING THE BATTERY ————

CLEANING YOUR BATTERY IS THE BEST WAY TO TAKE CARE OF IT, ALONG OTHER WAYS. YOU CAN CLEAN THE METAL TERMINALS WITH SANDPAPER AND THE CONNECTORS, CREATING A SOLID CONNECTION FOR THAT ELECTRICITY FLOW.

CHECKING THE BATTERY ——————

GETTING A FREE BATTERY TEST TO DETERMINE YOUR BATTERIES HEALTH IS A GOOD IDEA. USUALLY A GOOD CLEAN WILL DO THE JOB BUT IT DOESN'T HURT TO BE EXTRA CAUTIOUS. ALL IN ALL, IF THE CAR STARTS AND RUNS, MOST LIKELY IT IS WORKING AND IS SUFFICIENT ENOUGH. IT IS ALWAYS GOOD TO CHECK BEFORE EVERY WINTER SEASON SO YOU DON'T GET STRANDED!

SERPENTINE BELT CHECK ———

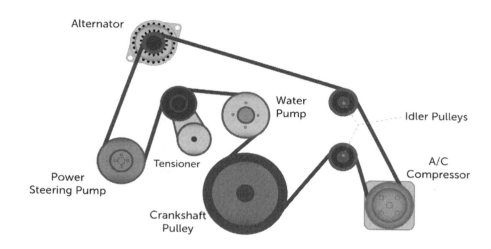

THIS IS YOUR SERPENTINE BELT SYSTEM. OF COURSE, EVERY SYSTEM IS DIFFERENT FOR DIFFERENT MANUFACTURERS. THIS DRIVES ALL YOUR ACCESSORIES LIKE YOUR ICE COLD AC IN THE SUMMER AND ENSURES YOUR CAR WORKS LIKE IT IS INTENDED TO.

SERPENTINE BELT CHECK ————

THE PURPOSE IS SIMPLE AND SO IS THE WAY TO CHECK THEM. IT IS A VERY INEXPENSIVE ITEM TO REPLACE BUT CATASTROPHIC IF IT BREAKS. ON MOST CARS IT WILL BE ON THE FRONT OR THE LEFT SIDE DEPENDING ON ENGINE CONFIGURATION.

SERPENTINE BELT CHECK ——

AS YOU SAW IN THE PICTURE ABOVE, THE LEFT ONE IS CRACKED AND WORN. ANY SIGNS OF CRACKS OR ABRASION ON THE SIDES, REPLACE IT. THESE CAN BE A PAIN TO REPLACE WITHOUT CERTAIN TOOLS, AND ROUTING THE BELT THROUGH. IF YOU THINK THE JOB IS SOMETHING YOU MIGHT NOT WANT TO TACKLE JUST YET, IT WOULD TAKE ANY SHOP NEXT TO 20-30 MINUTES.

CHECKING COOLANT ――――

ANTI-FREEZE OR COOLANT IS WHAT KEEPS YOUR CAR FROM GOING "BOOM!" AND DISSIPATES HEAT THROUGH PASSAGES IN THE ENGINE BLOCK AND THROUGH THE RADIATOR.

CHECKING COOLANT

THE COOLANT RESERVOIR (PICTURE ABOVE) IS WHAT HOLDS EXCESS COOLANT THAT ISN'T TAKEN UP BY YOUR ENGINE AND RADIATOR CAPACITY. ITS PURPOSE IS TO DISPLAY THE SYSTEMS FLUID LEVEL BY TWO MARKINGS ON THE PLASTIC CONTAINER. YOUR CAR MUST BE COOL BEFORE YOU REMOVE THE CAP, AS THE COOLING SYSTEM IS PRESSURIZED.

CHECKING
COOLANT —————

YOU MAY BE ASKING, WHAT IS THAT? WELL, THE MINIMUM MARKING IS FOR WHEN THE ENGINE IS COLD AND THE MAX LINE IS FOR WHEN THE ENGINE IS HOT. THE REASON IS BECAUSE OF HEAT EXPANSION. THE FLUID EXPANDS AND THAT GIVEN SPACE ALLOWS EXPANSION TO NOT OVERFLOW INTO THE ENGINE BAY, AND CORRODE ALMOST EVERY COPPER WIRE. AS COOLANT IS VERY DESTRUCTIVE TOWARDS ELECTRICAL COMPONENTS.

CHECKING
COOLANT

COOLANT FLOWS FROM THE TANK
TO THE RADIATOR, WHICH ALSO
USES AIRFLOW AND A FAN WHILE
IDLE TO KEEP THE COOLANT
TEMPERATURE DOWN, HENCE
KEEPING YOUR ENGINE COOL. IT IS
A SERIES OF FINS THAT AIR CAN
FLOW THROUGH AND IT IS LOCATED
AT THE FRONT OF YOUR VEHICLE.

CHECKING COOLANT ——————

ONE MORE THING TO CHECK FOR OTHER THAN HOW MUCH COOLANT, IS THE CONDITION. IF IT LOOKS DIRTY AND BROWN LIKE THIS IMAGE, THEN YOU BETTER REPLACE IT. YOU MAY BE WONDERING WHY, BUT COOLANT CAN CONDUCT ELECTRICITY WHEN IT IS CONTAMINATED.

CHECKING
COOLANT ——————

YOUR COOLANT CAN ALSO BE CHECKED
BY REMOVING THE RADIATOR CAP,
WHICH ISN'T AS ACCESSIBLE FOR
SOME CARS, WHICH IS WHY THE
RESERVOIR EXISTS. DO NOT REMOVE
THIS UNLESS YOUR CAR IS COOLED
DOWN, BECAUSE YOU DO NOT WANT TO
GET BURNING HOT COOLANT TO THE
FACE!

ENGINE OIL/DIPSTICK

ONE OF THE MOST VITAL THINGS TO KEEP YOUR ENGINE RUNNING, ENGINE OIL. WITHOUT IT YOUR ENGINE WOULD SEIZE AND NEVER MOVE AGAIN. ENGINE OIL IN SIMPLE TERMS LUBRICATES THE INTERNAL COMPONENTS OF THE ENGINE TO PREVENT METAL TO METAL CONTACT AND CREATE AN OIL PROTECTIVE LAYER.

ENGINE ─────────
OIL/DIPSTICK
- -

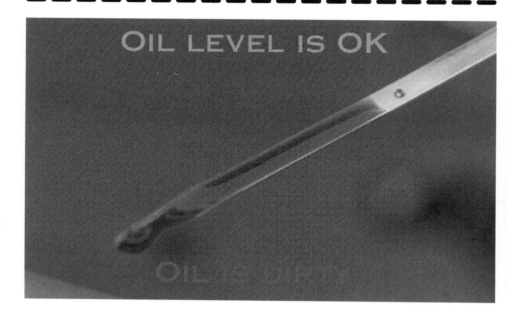

OIL LEVEL IS OK

IF YOU DECIDE YOU WANT TO
TACKLE AN OIL CHANGE THERE
ARE A FEW THINGS YOU NEED TO
KNOW ABOUT WHAT OIL IS AND
HOW IT IS CLASSIFIED. THE TERM
"5W-20" REFERS TO FLUID
VISCOSITY. "5W" MEANS HOW
THIN OR THICK THE OIL IS IN
COLD OR WARM CONDITIONS.

ENGINE OIL/DIPSTICK

WHEN THE ENGINE IS COLD, THE FLUID IS AT "5W" AND THE LOWER THE NUMBER, THE THINNER AND THE EASIER IT FLOWS THROUGH THE ENGINE. IN WINTER SEASON, YOU NEED THAT OIL TO FLOW AS FAST AS POSSIBLE AND WHEN THE ENGINE IS COLD, ESPECIALLY COLDER TEMPERATURES AS YOU KNOW, WILL USUALLY MAKE FLUIDS DENSER AND FLOW WILL BE COMPROMISED. NOW, WHEN YOUR ENGINE WARMS UP, IT WILL BECOME THICKER AND CREATE A PROTECTIVE LAYER THROUGH HEAT EXPANSION. EVERY INTERNAL ENGINE COMPONENT RIDES ON A THIN LAYER OF OIL. THE THICKER THE OIL GETS AS TEMPERATURE INCREASES, THE MORE PROTECTION. *NUDGE NUDGE*

ENGINE
OIL/DIPSTICK

JUST FOR REFERENCE, 5W-20 OIL WILL FLOW SLOWER THAN 0W-30 WHEN IT'S COLD, BUT 0W-30 WILL BE THICKER WHEN IT IS WARM.

ON A TYPICAL DIPSTICK, THERE WILL TWO HOLES OR DOTS. THE GOAL IS TO BE AT MINIMUM IN BETWEEN THOSE DOTS. PREFERABLY THE OIL "SHOULD" BE JUST BELOW OR TOUCHING THE TOP DOT OR HOLE IN THE DIPSTICK.

ENGINE OIL/DIPSTICK

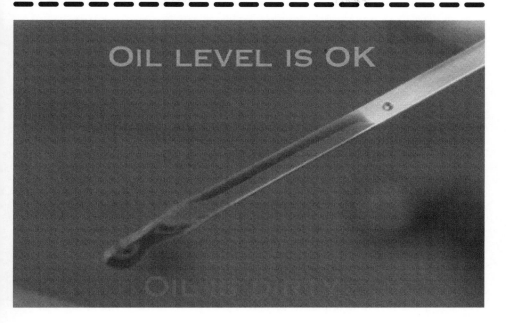

THE LAST THING IS, PLEASE PLEASE DO YOUR OIL CHANGES ON TIME. IF YOUR MANUFACTURER RECOMMENDS EVERY 8000KM OR JUST REGULAR MINERAL OIL, UPGRADE TO SYNTHETIC...YOU SHOULD REPLACE EVERY 5000KM (NON TURBO-CHARGED CARS) FOR THE ABSOLUTE BEST WAY TO KEEP YOUR ENGINE RUNNING BRAND NEW.

CHECKING BRAKE FLUID ────

WHAT IS BRAKE FLUID? IT IS WHAT MAKES YOU ABLE TO NOT HIT THE PERSON IN FRONT OF YOU USING YOUR BRAKING SYSTEM. YOU PROBABLY DONT REALIZE IT, BUT WITHOUT THE CAR ASSISTS WE HAVE TODAY, YOU WOULD NEED TWO FEET AND BREAK A SWEAT JUST TO STOP YOUR CAR. *JUST A FUN FACT*

CHECKING
BRAKE FLUID ⸺

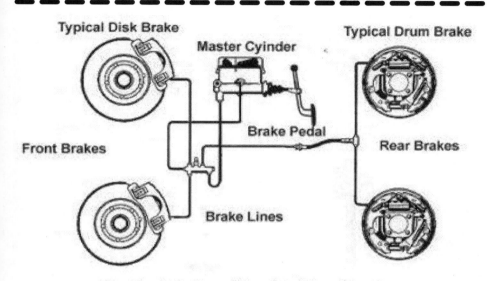

Typical Disk Brake   Master Cyinder   Typical Drum Brake

Front Brakes   Brake Pedal   Rear Brakes

Brake Lines

Typical Automotive Braking System

IN SUMMARY, THE BRAKE FLUID IS IN
A CLOSED, SEALED BRAKE SYSTEM, IT
GOES FROM THE MASTER CYLINDER,
THROUGH THE LINES AND FINALLY TO
THE CALIPERS. THIS WILL BE
EXPLAINED IN MORE DETAIL LATER.
ESSENTIALLY, WHY IS IT SO
IMPORTANT TO CHECK THIS?

CHECKING
BRAKE FLUID ———————

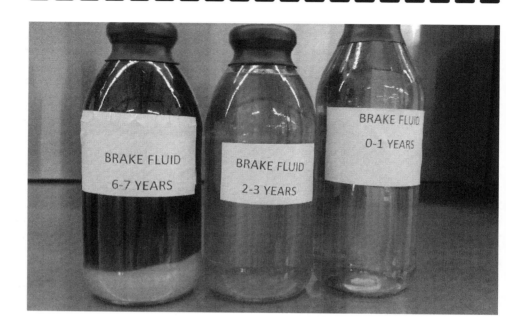

THE POINT IS, BRAKE FLUID CAN BECOME EXTREMELY CORROSIVE AND DAMAGE YOUR BRAKE LINES, WHICH WILL ALLOW AIR IN THE SYSTEM, THEREFORE YOUR BRAKES CAN POTENTIALLY OR WILL FAIL. THERE ARE CERTAIN SAFETY MEASURES TO PREVENT COMPLETE BRAKE FAILURE, BUT IT JUST ISN'T IDEAL.

CHECKING BRAKE FLUID ———

SO, THIS IS A BRAKE BOOSTER. WHEN YOU DEPRESS THE BRAKE PEDAL, THIS USES ENGINE VACUUM TO MAKE APPLYING THE BRAKES EFFORTLESS. THIS PUSHES THE BRAKE FLUID TO THE CALIPERS/DRUMS TO APPLY FRICTION TO THE ROTORS FROM THE PAD MATERIAL OR BRAKE SHOES.

CHECKING BRAKE FLUID ———

Brake fluid reservoir

ONCE YOU LOCATE THE BRAKE FLUID RESERVOIR, OPEN THE CAP AND CHECK FOR FLUID CONTAMINATION OR FLUID LEVEL. IT IS A SIMPLE AND QUICK CHECK, BUT IS VERY IMPORTANT! IF YOU HAVE A SOFT OR SPONGY PEDAL, YOU MOST LIKELY HAVE AIR IN THE SYSTEM AND WILL NEED TO BLEED YOUR BRAKES.

WINDSHIELD ——— WASHER FLUID

WINDSHIELD WASH IS REALLY EASY AND MORE IMPORTANT IN THE WINTER AS YOU HAVE SALT DEBRIS THAT GET ONTO YOUR WINDHSHIELD. WITHOUT IT, IT COULD BE DANGEROUS IF VISIBILITY IS COMPROMISED IF YOU HAPPEN TO RUN OUT OF IT WITH SALTY ROADS. (ITS HAPPENED, IT SUCKS)

WINDSHIELD —
WASHER FLUID

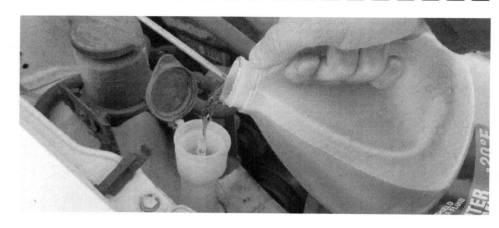

SIMPLY, JUST LOOK FOR THE WINDSHIELD FLUID TANK, WHICH IS LOCATED MOST LIKELY BY THE RADIATOR ON THE LEFT OR RIGHT WITH A SYMBOL THAT LOOKS LIKE THIS WITH A BLUE CAP:

WINDSHIELD ———
WASHER FLUID

JUST A FRIENDLY REMINDER
THAT IF IT'S EASY TO DO, JUST
DO IT! (NOT SPONSORED BY NIKE)

JUST FILL UP UNTIL FULL AND
YOU'LL BE GOOD TO GO.

WINDSHIELD WIPERS ———

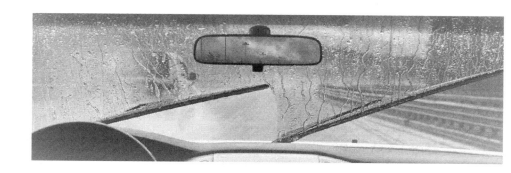

YOU DEFINITELY WON'T BE ABLE TO SEE WITHOUT GOOD WINDSHIELD WIPERS. IT IS CRUCIAL TO CHECK THEM BEFORE A BIG STORM HITS AND NOW THEY DONT WORK AS THEY'RE SUPPOSED TO. CHECKING THEM IS EASY AND EFFORTLESS. THEY CAN GET EXPENSIVE AS QUALITY GOES.

WINDSHIELD WIPERS ———

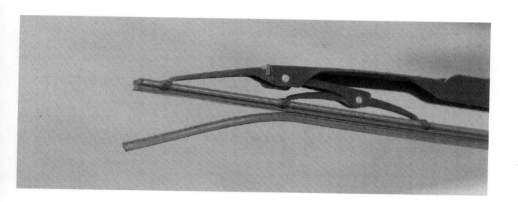

THE MOST COMMON DEFECT IS THAT THEY TEAR AND BECOME VERY INEFFICIENT, OR USELESS IN FACT. THIS HAPPENS USUALLY IN THE WINTER TIME BEING TORN OFF THE WINDSHIELD IN COLDER TEMPERATURES, IN ATTEMPT AT CLEANING THE WINDSHEILD OFF IN THE MORNING.

WINDSHIELD WIPERS ——————

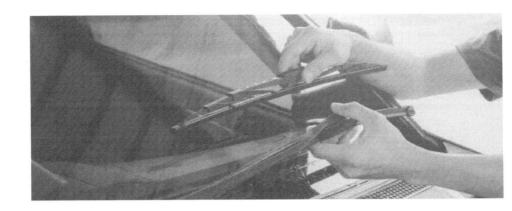

REPLACING THEM ISN'T THAT MUCH OF A TASK IF THEYRE AN OEM REPLACEMENT. USUALLY THEY HAVE A CLIP MECHANISM THAT CLICKS ON AND OFF WITH EASE. FOR UNIVERSAL OPTIONS, THERE ARE DIFFERENT ADAPTERS FOR ALL TYPES OF MANUFACTURERS.

CHECKING
YOUR TIRES ——————

IF YOU THINK ABOUT IT, THESE 4 PIECES OF CIRCULAR RUBBER ARE THE ONLY THINGS CONNECTING YOU TO THE ROAD, SO YOU BETTER CHOOSE WISELY WHAT YOU BUY! ALSO, CHECKING UP AND MAINTAINING THEM IS IMPORTANT.

CHECKING YOUR TIRES

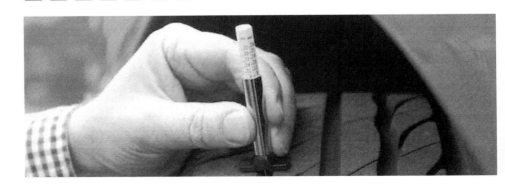

FIRST THINGS FIRST, TIRE DEPTH OR WEAR. THERE IS A TIME WHERE WORN TIRES CAN BECOME VERY UNSAFE AND NEED TO BE REPLACED. YOU MAY THINK YOU CAN GET ANOTHER SEASON OUT OF THEM, BUT EITHER A BLOWN TIRE OR EVEN HYDROPLANING IS POSSIBLE, AND VERY UNSAFE.

CHECKING
YOUR TIRES ━━━━━

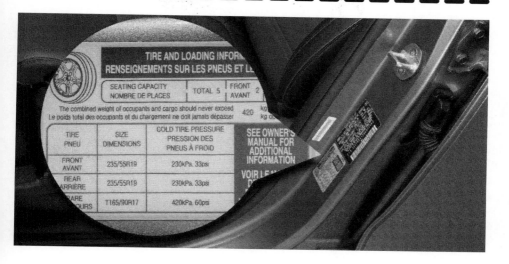

ALWAYS CHECK YOUR TIRE
DEPTH EITHER BY THE WEAR
INDICATORS OR A GAUGE.
NOW, THE NEXT THING IS TIRE
PRESSURE. MOST CARS RUN
35 PSI WHICH IS STANDARD.
HOW DOES TIRE PRESSURE
RELATE TO WEAR ON A TIRE?
OH! GOOD THING YOU ASKED.

CHECKING YOUR TIRES

YOU CAN FIND THE PRESSURE REQUIRED INSIDE YOUR DRIVER DOOR ON A LABEL. TIRE PRESSURE ALONG WITH YOUR SUSPENSION KEEPS A COMFY RIDE WITH AIR ABSORBING ANY BUMPS, ASSISTING THE CARS SUSPENSION AS WELL. IF YOU HAVE UNDER-INFALTED TIRES, THEY CAN WEAR UNEVENLY WHICH THEY WILL WEAR OUT FASTER. YOU CAN CHECK TIRE PRESSURE WITH AN INEXPENSIVE PRESSURE GAUGE.

CHECKING YOUR TIRES

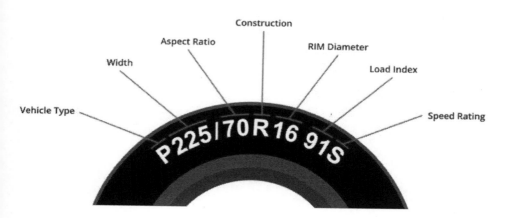

Construction
Aspect Ratio
RIM Diameter
Width
Load Index
Vehicle Type
Speed Rating

P225/70R16 91S

I KNOW IF YOU HAVE BOUGHT NEW TIRES BEFORE, YOU'RE WONDERING WHAT ALL THESE NUMBERS MEAN? YOU WON'T NEED TO WORRY ABOUT MOST OF THESE NUMBERS YET, UNLESS YOU'RE LOOKING FOR HIGH PERFORMANCE APPLICATIONS.

CHECKING YOUR TIRES ————

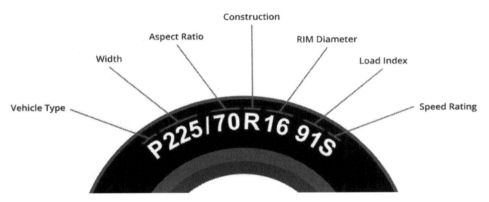

Vehicle Type — Width — Aspect Ratio — Construction — RIM Diameter — Load Index — Speed Rating

P225/70R16 91S

"225/70R16" ARE THE MOST IMPORTANT DIGITS HERE.

225- WIDTH OF THE TIRE IN MILLIMETRES. (SIDE TO SIDE)
70 - SIZE OF SIDEWALL IN MILLIMETRES. (HOLE TO TOP OF TIRE)
R16- SIZE OF THE RIM IN INCHES

YOU CANNOT FOT A 17" RIM ON A 16" SIZED TIRE!

CHECKING
YOUR TIRES ‗‗‗‗

A FINAL TIP FOR MAINTAINING YOUR TIRES ARE CHECKING BETWEEN SEASON AND TEMPERATURE CHANGES. THE AIR EXPANDS AND CONTRACTS INSIDE YOUR TIRE WHICH WILL AFFECT YOUR TIRE PRESSURE, ESPECIALLY BETWEEN SUMMER AND WINTER!

BRAKE PAD AND ROTORS

ONE OF THE MOST IMPORTANT SYSTEMS IN YOUR CAR, YOUR BRAKES! THIS WILL TEACH YOU A FEW WAYS TO CHECK THEM FOR WEAR AND MAYBE HOW LONG THEY WILL LAST! REPLACING THEM FOR THE FIRST TIME CAN BE CONFUSING, BUT WE WILL WORRY ABOUT THAT ANOTHER TIME.

BRAKE PAD AND ROTORS

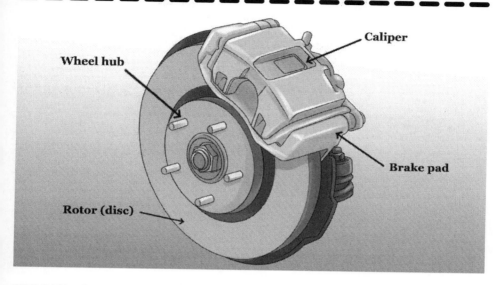

Caliper

Wheel hub

Brake pad

Rotor (disc)

THE COMPONENTS IN YOUR TYPICAL BRAKE SYSTEM WILL BE THE BRAKE ROTOR, BRAKE PADS, AND YOUR BRAKE CALIPER. ESSENTIALLY, THE CALIPER USES HYDRAULIC PRESSURE TO ALLOW THE BRAKE PAD TO CREATE FRICTION ON THE ROTOR SURFACE, HENCE SLOWING DOWN THE VEHICLE.

BRAKE PAD AND ROTORS

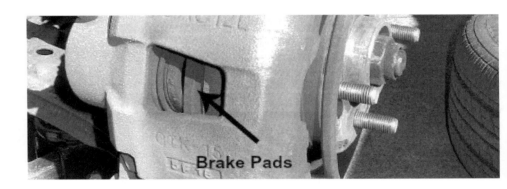

Brake Pads

THE EASIEST WAY TO CHECK YOUR BRAKE PADS ARE THROUGH THE INSPECTION HOLE ON YOUR CALIPER. SOME CARS MAY BE DIFFERENT BUT THE OUTSIDE PAD IS USUALLY VISIBLE TO INSPECT. IF YOU WANT TO KNOW HOW MUCH MATERIAL IS LEFT, YOU CAN BUY A BRAKE PAD GAUGE WHICH TELLS YOU HOW THICK THEY ARE IN MM.

BRAKE PAD AND ROTORS

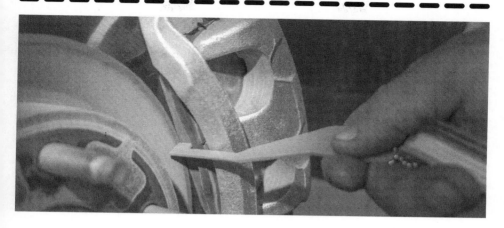

HERE IS A QUICK IMAGE ON HOW TO USE THIS GAUGE, IF YOU WERE SO CURIOUS ON HOW GOOD YOUR BRAKES ARE. THE COLORED FINS ON THE GAUGE HAVE A LIP ON THE END WHICH MUST FIT SNUG IN BETWEEN THE PAD AND AGAINST THE ROTOR. GREEN IS GOOD, YELLOW IS OKAY, AND RED MEANS REPLACE ASAP. THE SAME AS GREEN MEANS FLOOR IT!

BRAKE PAD AND ROTORS

NOW, CHECKING YOUR ROTOR IS EVEN MORE SIMPLE! JUST LOOK FOR RUST BUILD-UP, OR ANY HEAT CRACKS. YOU CAN ALSO MEASURE THE THICKNESS OF THE ROTOR AND FIND THE SPECIFICATIONS, BUT THAT'S ONLY FOR NERDS. THE RULE OF THUMB IS THAT A ROTOR TYPICALLY CAN LAST FOR TWO PAD REPLACEMENTS BEFORE REPLACING ANOTHER PAD AND ROTOR COMBO WITH EXTRA SAUCE ON THE SIDE.

BRAKE PAD AND ROTORS ————

IF YOUR CAR HAS A WEIRD PULSE FEELING WHENEVER YOU PRESS THE BRAKE PEDAL, YOU MOST LIKELY HAVE A WARPED BRAKE ROTOR. THIS USUALLY HAPPENS AS THEY WEAR OR IF THEY WERE BEING EXPOSED TO AN EXCESSIVE AMOUNT OF HEAT, WHICH IN FACT WILL WARP THEM. THIS CAN HAPPEN FROM A SEIZED CALIPER. IF THE BRAKES ARE ALWAYS CAUSING FRICTION, THE BY-PRODUCT IS HEAT, AND A LOT OF IT! IF YOU ALSO HEAR A SQUEAKY NOISE, YOU MOST LIKELY HAVE LOW BRAKE PADS OR YOU WILL NEED A BRAKE SERVICE. A SERIVCE IS JUST RE-LUBRICATING THE SURFACES WHICH THE PADS RIDE ON AND A CLEANING OF ANY RUST. ALSO RE-SURFACING THE PADS FOR ANY GLAZING.

CHAPTER 2: THINGS EVERY DRIVER SHOULD KNOW

THIS WILL BE SOMETHING THAT EVERY DRIVER OR NEW CAR PERSON SHOULD KNOW. IN THIS CHAPTER YOU WILL BE LEARNING HOW TO:

1. HOW TO OPEN YOUR HOOD
2. HOW TO JACK UP YOUR CAR
3. HOW TO CHANGE A TIRE
4. DOING YOUR OWN WORK ADVICE

OPENING YOUR HOOD

FIRST THINGS FIRST, FINDING THE HOOD RELEASE BUTTON OR LEVER. IT IS USUALLY LOCATED UNDER YOUR DASH TO THE LEFT, OR EVEN NEAR THE FLOOR BY YOUR LEFT FOOT. JUST PULL THE RELEASE LEVER LABELED CLEARLY, AND PULL UNTIL YOU HEAR YOUR HOOD RELEASE.

OPENING YOUR HOOD

FINDING THE HOOD LATCH IS THE HARDEST PART, UNTIL YOU HAVE DONE IT A FEW TIMES. THEY EITHER CAN BE IN THE MIDDLE OR MOST LIKELY TO THE LEFT OF THE FRONT OF YOUR CAR. THERE ARE TWO COMMON DESIGNS; EITHER A VERTICAL RELEASE (IMAGE ABOVE) OR A HORIZONTAL RELEASE.

OPENING YOUR HOOD

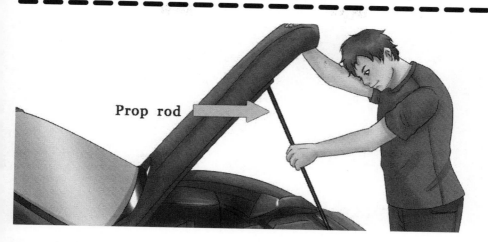

Prop rod

NOW, ONCE RELEASED THE HOOD WILL POP UP, AND NOW JUST LIFT THE HOOD SAFELY WHILE LOCATING YOUR HOOD SUPPORT BAR. USUALLY, IT IS JUST A METAL ROD WITH A HOOKED END THAT YOU CAN PLACE INTO A DESIGNATED AREA UNDER YOUR HOOD TO SUPPORT IT PROPERLY.

JACKING UP YOUR CAR

JACKING UP YOUR CAR IS ALL ABOUT SAFETY, AND DOING IT PROPERLY. UNLESS YOU'RE ON THE SIDE OF THE ROAD AND ONLY HAVE THOSE LITTLE PUNY JACKS THAT COME WITH YOUR SPARE TIRE, I WOULD RECOMMEND USING A 1-2 TON CAR JACK TO MAKE THINGS EASIER.

JACKING UP YOUR CAR

NO MATTER WHAT JACK YOU'RE USING, THE TYPICAL SPOT THAT YOU SHOULD LIFT ON A CAR ARE JUST BESIDE YOUR WHEELS OR CALLED THE "ROCKERS". IT IS JUST A DOUBLE STACKED PIECE OF WELDED METAL FOR STURDINESS TO SUPPORT THE CARS WEIGHT.

JACKING UP YOUR CAR

ALWAYS MAKE SURE TO CHOCK YOUR WHEELS BEFORE LIFTING YOUR CAR AND MAKE SURE THE CAR IS IN PARK ALSO WITH THE HANDBRAKE APPLIED, FOR MANUAL TRANSMISSIONS ALSO. YOU CAN ALSO LEAVE IT IN FIRST GEAR FOR EXTRA SAFETY.

JACKING UP YOUR CAR

ONCE EVERYTHING FOR SAFETY IS DONE, YOU CAN NOW PLACE THE JACK IN THE CORRECT POSITION UNDER YOUR CAR. ALWAYS MAKE SURE EVERYTHING IS LINED UP BEFORE LIFTING THE CAR OFF THE GROUND.

JACKING UP
YOUR CAR

ONCE THE CAR IS OFF THE GROUND TO YOUR LIKING, ALWAYS USE A JACK STAND (1-2 TON) TO SUPPORT THE VEHICLE. LOWER THE CAR, AND FOR EVEN MORE SAFETY, KEEP THE CAR JACK SNUG AGAINST THE BOTTOM OF THE CAR BESIDE THE JACK FOR EXTRA SUPPORT.

CHANGING A TIRE

CHANGING A TIRE IS VERY IMPORTANT IN SAVING MONEY AND FOR REGULAR MAINTENANCE. KNOWING THIS COULD ALSO SAVE YOU IF YOUR TIRE WERE TO BLOW IN THE MIDDLE OF NOWHERE!

CHANGING A TIRE

BEFORE JACKING THE CAR UP, IT WOULD MAKE LIFE EASIER IF YOU DON'T HAVE A POWERFUL IMPACT GUN TO LOOSEN THE LUG NUTS BEFORE LIFTING THE CAR. ONCE YOU LIFT IT, THEY SHOULD COME OFF WITH JUST YOUR HAND STRENGTH.

CHANGING A TIRE

IF YOU HAVEN'T ALREADY, GO READ "HOW TO JACK UP YOUR CAR" SECTION IN THIS BOOK. PG 58-62

ONCE THE CAR IS IN THE AIR, LOOSEN ALL THE LUG NUTS FROM THE WHEEL. SOME CARS MAY HAVE A WHEEL COVER OR HUB COVER WHICH WILL NEED TO BE REMOVED TO ACCESS THE LUG NUTS.

CHANGING A TIRE

IF YOUR WHEEL IS SEIZED ONTO THE HUB, HERE ARE A FEW TRICKS TO GET IT OFF WITH EASE.

GET A RUBBER MALLET (PREFERABLY) AND HIT THE BACKSIDE OF THE TIRE TO KNOCK IT OFF THE HUB. OR TRY PRYING ON IT WITH TWO HANDS AND PULL TO THE OUTSIDE OF THE CAR.

CHANGING A TIRE

ONCE THE TIRE IS OFF, THIS IS A GOOD TIME TO INSPECT THE BRAKES AND ANYTHING BEHIND THE WHEEL THAT ISNT VISIBLE. ITS RECOMMENDED TO CLEAN THE ROTOR MOUNTING SURFACE IF THERE IS A SIGNIFICANT AMOUNT OF RUST BUILD-UP BEFORE INSTALLING A WHEEL BACK ON.

CHANGING A TIRE

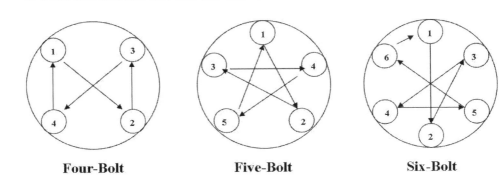

Four-Bolt   Five-Bolt   Six-Bolt

DEPENDING ON YOUR BOLT PATTERN, YOU NEED TO FOLLOW A SPECIFIC PATTERN TO TORQUING OR INSTALLING THE LUG NUTS FOR PROPER FITMENT. FOR A 5 STAR PATTERN, TORQUE IN A PATTERN OF A STAR, TO MAKE SURE ALL SIDES OF THE WHEEL ARE INSTALLED EVENLY. PURCHASING A TORQUE WRENCH AT THE MINIMUM WOULD BE IDEAL.

CHANGING A TIRE ————————

YOU SHOULD SNUG UP ALL OF THEM VERY LIGHTLY THEN TIGHTEN THEM MORE USING THE PATTERNS BUT NOT TOO TIGHT YET. ONCE THAT IS DONE YOU CAN LOWER THE CAR BACK ONTO THE GROUND. GET A TORQUE WRENCH AND FIND THE CERTAIN SPECIFICATION FOR YOUR CAR, WHICH CAN BE FOUND IN YOUR OWNERS MANUAL OR ONLINE TYPICALLY. THIS IS THE ONLY ONE THING I WOULD STRESS TO PLEASE PUT INTO GOOD PRACTICE. ONLY USE YOUR OWN STRENGTH TO TIGHTEN WHEEL LUG NUTS IN EMERGENCY SITUATIONS.

CHANGING A
TIRE

FINALLY, MOST CARS USE 100 FT.LBS ON A TORQUE WRENCH BUT DONT ASSUME THAT FOR EVERY CAR. TORQUING IS THE LAST STEP BUT YOU SHOULD RE-TORQUE THEM AFTER 500 KM OR SO JUST IN CASE.

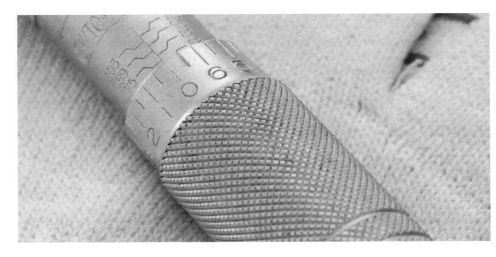

THE FINAL THING YOU SHOULD KNOW IS HOW TO READ OR ADJUST A TORQUE WRENCH PROPERLY.

CHANGING A TIRE

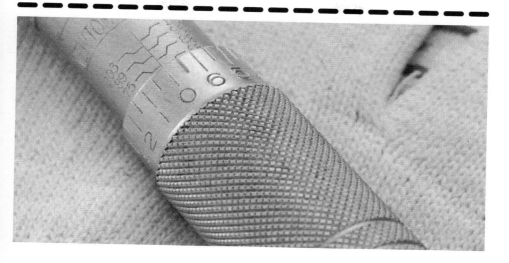

MOST TORQUE WRENCHES ARE THE SAME, BUT MOST GO UP BY 10 FT.LBS AND EVERY FULL TURN IS 10 FT.LBS UP THE SCALE. IF YOU WANT TO GO UP TO 100 FT.LBS YOU WOULD NEED TO START AT 0 AND UNLOCK THE WHEEL TO TURN IT. AS FAR AS NUMBERS GO, YOU WOULD NEED TO ROTATE IT 10 TIMES TO REACH 100 FT.LBS.

CHANGING A TIRE

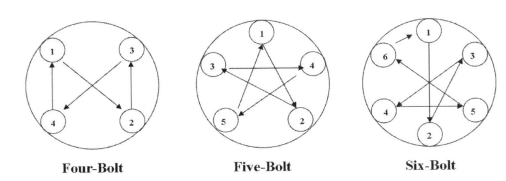

Four-Bolt   Five-Bolt   Six-Bolt

AFTER YOU SET YOUR TORQUE WRENCH AND TORQUE THEM IN A STAR PATTERN, MAKE SURE TO RE-CHECK IN A CIRCULAR PATTERN. SOMETIMES, THE FIRST ONE YOU STARTED ON CAN BE SLIGHTLY LOOSE AND ONE LAST CHECK WILL ONLY TAKE 20 SECONDS OR LESS. IT WOULDN'T HURT TO CHECK YOUR TIRE PRESSURE WHILE YOU'RE THERE.

DIY MAINTENANCE TIPS

IF YOU WERE TO DO YOUR OWN OIL CHANGE OR COOLANT FLUSH, ALWAYS DISPOSE OF FLUIDS PROPERLY. ALMOST ANY REPAIR SHOP TAKES FLUIDS AND RECYCLE THEM FOR FREE. ONCE YOU FINISH THE REPAIR OR JOB, STORE THE FLUIDS IN CONTAINER(S) AND BRING THEM TO BE DISPOSED FOR YOU.

ALWAYS USE A JACK STAND FOR ANY REASON TO LIFT THE VEHCILE OR WORKING UNDER IT. A JACK HAS A POSSIBILITY OF FAILING AND THAT WILL RESULT IN SERIOUS INJURY. YOU CAN NEVER BE TOO SAFE.

TRY TO AVOID WORKING ON THINGS THAT ARE HOT, AS THERE IS A CHANCE OF GETTING BURNED FROM HOT ENGINE COMPONENTS.

IF YOU WERE GONNA TORQUE ANYTHING, ALWAYS TORQUE YOU R WHEELS OR LUG NUTS CORRECTLY. TIGHTENING THEM TOO MUCH CAN WEAKEN THE STUDS OR TOO LOSE MAY RESULT IN A LOST WHEEL AT HIGH SPEED.

THANKS FOR
READING!

MY GOAL HERE IS TO HOPE YOU HAVE LEARNED SOMETHING NEW WHILE READING THIS BOOK, AND NOW YOU ARE MORE KNOWLEDGEABLE IN MAINTAINING YOUR CAR THAN YOU WERE BEFORE!

Printed in Great Britain
by Amazon